Motivational Quotes for Weight Loss

Weight Loss Inspiration for the Motivationally-Challenged

Emma J. Adams

First Printing, 2012

Printed in the United States of America

Liability Disclaimer

By reading this book, you assume all risks associated with using the advice given below, with a full understanding that you, solely, are responsible for anything that may occur as a result of putting this information into action in any way, and regardless of your interpretation of the advice.

You further agree that our company cannot be held responsible in any way for the success or failure of your business as a result of the information presented in this book. It is your responsibility to conduct your own due diligence regarding the safe and successful operation of your business if you intend to apply any of our information in any way to your business operations.

Terms of Use

You are given a non-transferable, "personal use" license to this book. You cannot distribute it or share it with other individuals.

Also, there are no resale rights or private label rights granted when purchasing this book. In other words, it's for your own personal use only.

Motivational Quotes for Weight Loss

Weight Loss Inspiration for the Motivationally-Challenged

Table of Contents

Preface

HOME COOKING WITHOUT THE HASSLES

Weight Loss Inspiration

Weight loss is a national obsession in the United States. With 68% of American adults falling into the overweight category – and 33.8% into the obese ranks by body mass index, we have a problem.

Yes, a big one.

Not surprisingly, weight loss and dieting are the sport of the hour for many of us trying to get back to a normal weight. While there are many diet books out there, there are relatively fewer resources for people who recognize that they need help with motivation.

As with any habit change, dieting and weight loss take time, effort, and perseverence. The purpose of this book is to help you along, day by day, to make the changes you need to make.

With a little weight loss inspiration to guide you along each day, you can reach your goals and maintain the healthier lifestyle you deserve. This book is a collection of motivational quotes of the day, with images, for people on a weight loss program. Mixed in, you will find funny quotes and images to give you a laugh and a little perspective – that is how to cope with the inevitable ups and downs you may experience along the way.

You can use these moments of inspiration in whatever way works best for you – to start your day, end your day, copy into your journal or diary, post on your refrigerator or computer screensaver.

 If you need practical tips, ideas, and information on how to stick to a diet, get our companion guide book, *How to Stick to a Diet: Weight Loss Tips for Women (available onliine paperback and digital book version at major retailers such as Amazon).*

This book here is your weight loss buddy, your cheering section, your supporter. Purely motivation, reminders, and inspiration to stay with your program, whatever diet plan you are following. Because you matter.

Let's get started...

Inspiration Day 1

"It is never too late to be who you might have been."

- George Eliot

Inspiration Day 2

"I'm a great believer in luck, and I find the harder I work, the more I have of it."

- Thomas Jefferson

Inspiration Day 3

"Even if you're on the right track, you'll get run over
if you just sit there."

- Will Rogers

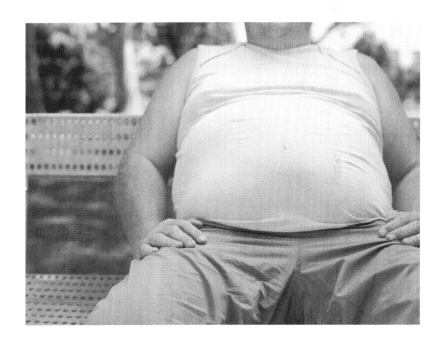

Inspiration Day 4

"People know you for what you've done, not for
what you plan to do."

- Author Unknown

Inspiration Day 5

"I try to take one day at a time, but sometimes, several days attack me at once."

- Jennifer Yane

Inspiration Day 6

"My doctor told me to stop having intimate dinners for four. Unless there are three other people."

- Orson Welles

Inspiration Day 7

"Where do you go to get anorexia?"

- Shelley Winters

Inspiration Day 8

"Stress spelled backwards is desserts. Coincidence?
I think not!"

- Author Unknown

Inspiration Day 9

"A man can stand a lot as long as he
can stand himself."

- Axel Munthe

Inspiration Day 10

"I've been on a constant diet for the last two decades. I've lost a total of 789 pounds. By all accounts, I should be hanging from a charm bracelet."

- Erma Bombeck

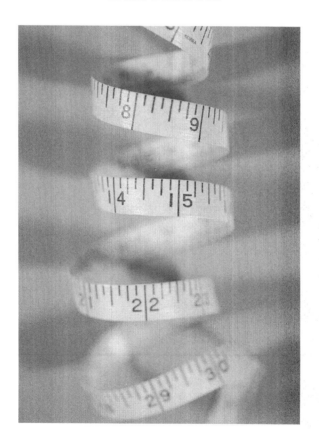

Inspiration Day 11

"I know of no more encouraging fact than the unquestionable ability of man to elevate his life by a conscious endeavor."

- Henry David Thoreau

Inspiration Day 12

"By failing to prepare, you are preparing to fail."

- Benjamin Franklin

Inspiration Day 13

"Never tell people how to do things. Tell them what to do and they will surprise you with their ingenuity."

- George S. Patton

Inspiration Day 14

"Sometimes the best helping hand you can get is a good, firm push."

- Joann Thomas

Inspiration Day 15

"After all the trouble you go to, you get about as much actual 'food' out of eating an artichoke as you would from llicking 30-40 postage stamps."

- Miss Piggy

Inspiration Day 16

"You may not be responsible for getting knocked down, but you're certainly esponsible for getting back up."

- Wally Amos

Inspiration Day 17

"It's bizarre that the produce manager is more important to my children's health than the pediatrician."

- Meryl Streep

Inspiration Day 18

"When baking, follow directions. When cooking, go by your own taste."

- Laiko Bahrs

Inspiration Day 19

"Worries go down better with soup."

- Jewish Proverb

Inspiration Day 20

"I never had a policy; I have just tried to do my very best each and every day."

- Abraham Lincoln

Inspiration Day 21

"You can outdistance that which is running after you,
but not what is running inside you."

- Rwandan Proverb

Inspiration Day 22

"They cannot take away our self-respect if we do not give it to them."

- Mahatma Gandhi

Inspiration Day 23

"Food is an important part of a balanced diet."

- Fran Lebowitz

Inspiration Day 24

"The willingness to accept responsibility for one's own life is the source from which self-respect springs."

- Joan Didion

Inspiration Day 25

"I've failed over and over and over again in my life, and that is why I succeed."

- Michael Jordan

Inspiration Day 26

"The part can never be well unless the whole is well."

- Plato

Inspiration Day 27

"A hard beginning maketh a good ending."

- John Heywood

Inspiration Day 28

"Mountains cannot be surmounted except by winding paths."

- Johann Wolfgang Von Goethe

Inspiration Day 29

"Your only obligation in any lifetime is to be true to yourself."

- Richard Bach

Inspiration Day 30

"You cannot change your destination overnight, but you can change your direction overnight."

- Jim Rohn

Inspiration Day 31

"The leading cause of death among fashion models is falling through street grates."

- Dave Barry

Inspiration Day 32

"Everyone thinks of changing the world, but no one thinks of changing himself."

- Leo Tolstoy

Inspiration Day 33

"Forget about the consequences of failure. Failure is only a temporary change in direction to set you straight for your next success."

- Denis Waitley

Inspiration Day 34

"When fate hands us a lemon, let's try
to make lemonade."

- Dale Carnegie

Inspiration Day 35

"Nothing is so fatiguing as the eternal hanging on of an uncompleted task."

- William James

Inspiration Day 36

"You get what you think about, whether you want it
or not. Commit to thinking about what you want,
rather than how impossible or difficult
that dream may seem."

- Dr. Wayne W. Dyer

Inspiration Day 37

"If and When were planted, and Nothing grew."

- Proverb

Inspiration Day 38

"It is health which is real wealth, not pieces of silver and gold."

- Gandhi

Inspiration Day 39

"You must do the thing you think you cannot do."

- Eleanor Roosevelt

Inspiration Day 40

"Beginnings are only difficult without any action."

- Byron Pulsifer

Inspiration Day 41

"Laughter gives us distance. It allows us to step back
from an event, deal with it, and then move on."

- Bob Newhart

Inspiration Day 42

"Never lose hope no matter how long it takes! Believe in yourself even when you feel alone in your battles."

- Shadonna Richards

Inspiration Day 43

"Health and cheerfulness naturally beget each other."

- Joseph Addison

Inspiration Day 44

"The secret of getting ahead is getting started."

- Sally Berger

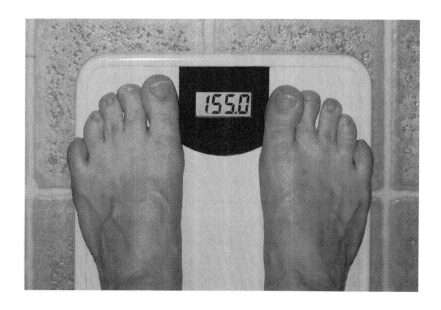

Inspiration Day 45

"In time of test, family is best."

- Burmese Proverb

Inspiration Day 46

"All our dreams can come true, if we have
the courage to pursue them."

- Walt Disney

Inspiration Day 47

"Once you choose hope, anything's possible."

- Christopher Reeve

Inspiration Day 48

"Eat well, drink in moderation, and sleep sound, in these three good health abound."

- Latin Proverb

Inspiration Day 49

"In the confrontation between the stream and the rock, the stream always wins – not through strength, but by perseverence."

- H. Jackson Brown

Inspiration Day 50

"Success is steady progress toward
one's personal goals."

- Jim Rohn

Inspiration Day 51

"You only grow when you are alone."

- Paul Newman

Inspiration Day 52

"The biggest secret in life is that there is no big secret. Whatever your goal, you can get there if you're
willing to work at it."

- Oprah Winfrey

Inspiration Day 53

"You see, in life, lots of people know what to do, but few people actually do what they know. Knowing is not enough! You must take action."

- Tony Robbins

Inspiration Day 54

"You can do it if you believe you can."

- Napoleon Hill

Inspiration Day 55

"Hope is the dream of a soul awake."

- French Proverb

Inspiration Day 56

"God will not look you over for medals, degrees, or diplomas, but for scars."

- Elbert Hubbard

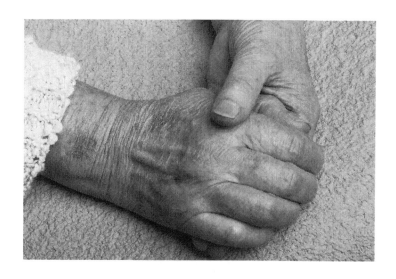

Inspiration Day 57

"It always seems impossible until it's done."

- Nelson Mandela

Inspiration Day 58

"If your happiness depends on what somebody else does, I guess you do have a problem."

- Richard Bach

Inspiration Day 59

"It is not the mountain we conquer but ourselves."

- Edmund Hillary

Inspiration Day 60

"Opportunity doesn't wait for convenience."

- Anna Olson

Inspiration Day 61

"You will never be happy if you continue to search for what happiness consists of. You will never live if you are looking for the meaning of life."

- Albert Camus

Inspiration Day 62

"Perseverence is not a long race; it is many short rac-
es one after the other."

- Walter Elliot

Inspiration Day 63

"Believe in yourself! Have faith in your abilities!
Without a humble but reasonable confidence in your
own powers you cannot be successful or happy."

- Norman Vincent Peale

Inspiration Day 64

"The most painful thing to experience is not defeat, but regret."

- Leo Buscaglia

Inspiration Day 65

"We were born to succeed, not to fail."

- William Barclay

Inspiration Day 66

"You have to learn the rules of the game. And then
you have to play better than anyone else."

- Albert Einstein

Inspiration Day 67

"To be without some of the things you want is an indis-
pensable part of happiness."

- Bertrand Russell

Inspiration Day 68

"Our bodies are our gardens –
our wills are our gardeners."

- William Shakespeare

Inspiration Day 69

"Success doesn't come to you – you go to it."

- Marva Collins

Inspiration Day 70

"Every day is an opportunity to make
a new happy ending."

- Author Unknown

Inspiration Day 71

"Take care of your body. It's the only place you have to live."

- Jim Rohn

Inspiration Day 72

"High achievement always take place in the frame-
work of high expectation."

- Charles F. Kettering

Inspiration Day 73

"It is no use saying, 'We are doing our best.' You have got to succeed in doing what is necessary."

- Winston Churchill

Inspiration Day 74

"The greatest wealth is health."

- Virgil

Inspiration Day 75

"A moment on the lips, a lifetime on the hips."

- Author Unknown

Inspiration Day 76

"People often say that motivation doesn't last.
Well, neither does bathing - that's why we
recommend it daily."

- Zig Ziglar

Inspiration Day 77

"Only those who will risk going too far can possibly find out how far one can go."

- T.S. Eliot

A Fable of Big Change

Carly Caterpillar led a happy life. Food was plentiful and she enjoyed the company of many friends.

One day she was feeling very sleepy. She made a cozy cocoon, climbed in, and went to sleep.

When she awoke, she felt different somehow. *"Wow,"* she thought. *"I'm really skinny! I must have been asleep a long time."*

As she crawled out of her cocoon, she discovered all kinds of changes!

One after another, the changes became apparent and Carly was *not* happy at all! First of all, there were these things sticking out of her back that got in the way in tight spaces. Then she had to learn how to walk all over again, with only 6 long, thin legs.

She was also hungry, and took a big bite of a nearby leaf. *"What happened to the leaves?"* she said. *"They taste nasty! And where are all my friends?"*

Sad and frustrated, Carly felt like a misfit in a new world.

And then came the accident!

A sudden gust of wind pushed her off the tree. *"Oh, no-o-o-o-o-o!"* she cried out. Down, down she fell. Then, just as she was sure she was going to plummet to her death, she wiggled her wings and soared! She sailed gracefully around the tree toward the meadow.

There, to her surprise, were her friends! Their bright colors blended in with the abundant blooms of the many flowers, but she was still able to recognize all of her friends.

"Carly! Taste this lovely nectar!" they exclaimed. She tasted it and, to her surprise, it *delicious!* She flitted from flower to flower, enjoying the many new flavors.

Then, with her friends, Carly blissfully flew away to new lands. She had many wonderful adventures and realized how lucky she was to have transformed from a plain green caterpillar into the beautiful butterfly she was.

When unexpected changes happen in our lives, our first reaction is often panic. Like Carly, we tend to hold onto the past and resist change, especially if we're content with the way things are. The bigger the change, the more we push against it, making it harder on ourselves in the process.

However, change is inevitable. As we travel on our journey, we must learn and grow, and change gives us a chance to do just that. ***Otherwise we would stagnate!***

If you find yourself having a hard time accepting new situations, you may be letting a fear of the unknown stop you from seeing the new opportunities you've been given.

Whenever one door closes in your life, another one always opens. Are you afraid to look inside?

Do you imagine all the bad things that can come of it? What about the wonderful new experiences waiting on the other side?

If you focus on finding the good, you'll be able to take advantage of what's through that open door.

For example, what if you lost your job? Such a change would naturally be devastating, at least at first. But would it really be the end of the world? Have you considered the possibility that the job loss could be the one thing that leads you to the career of your dreams?

You may find another job with higher pay and better benefits, or perhaps it would lead you to start your own successful business. How wonderful this would be!

There are many changes in your life that can lead to greater fulfillment. For example, true love, marriage, and having a child all require drastic changes, and they may be scary at first, but just think of the whole new world of wonderful possibilities!

So embrace change and seek its opportunities. When you do, life will embrace you with its splendor.

Self-Reflection Questions:

- What changes in my life brought new, exciting, benefits?
- Did I resist the differences in my life as these changes occurred?
- How can I develop a more positive attitude about change?

10 Words to Motivate Yourself to Keep Going

No matter where you are in your progress toward your weight loss goal, setbacks can occur and can cause disappointment and a loss of momentum.

Your efforts can seem emotionally or psychologically draining from time to time.

To boost your confidence, **here's a list of the top 10 power words and tips to keep you motivated and passionate, no matter what life throws your way. Use these in your daily meditation or just to remind you that you can succeed:**

1. **Purpose.** Whenever you're feeling discouraged or disappointed, always remember your original purpose. Reminding yourself of the original reason for venturing down your path in the first place will help refresh your mind when things go awry.

2. **Planning.** Though you may think that you've done enough planning towards the fulfillment of your goal,

thinking it through again will help eliminate aspects of your plan of action that may be causing you setbacks. Put all your thoughts down on paper, from the smallest details to the larger movements.

- Being able to see the timeline of your mission will help you focus on taking one step at a time to reach your goals.

3. **Acceptance.** Accepting that you're a human being who's bound to have ups and downs is absolutely crucial to your success. Without this self-acceptance, you'll be subject to a foggy mind that's unable to think positively, clearly, and innovatively.

- *Acceptance of what hasn't worked in the past helps you gain a better knowledge of what will work in the future.*

4. **Reward.** When your motivation starts to wean, it's crucial to give yourself rewards along the way. This is one of the best ways to stay motivated on your path to success.

By giving yourself a taste of what you're working for – whether it's financial freedom, career responsibility, or your dream lifestyle – you won't feel like you're working so hard for nothing. This refreshes your mind and helps you work more productively.

5. **Health.** You know what this entails: moderate exercise, a healthy diet, and 7-8 hours of sleep per night. Feeling worn-down will make it almost impossible to pursue

your goals and vision with the same clarity and vigor you had when you first set out.

- *Take care of your basic needs first, and you'll be strong enough to pursue your dreams.*

6. **Motivation.** Research motivational books, CDs, and seminars. Sometimes hearing motivational tips from a different perspective can greatly motivate you to act and succeed.

   - Find a source or two that touches you in some way and keep them close for those moments when you feel discouraged. After all, we all get discouraged at one time or another.

7. **Organization.** Ever feel depressed and worn out, and then you clean your surroundings and instantly feel more focused and motivated? The same applies to your goal. Organize and clean house when it comes to the operation of your goal.

   - *Organizing yourself gives you a fresh start and a feeling of clarity.* In doing so, you'll be able to attack your short and long-term goals more vigorously and effectively.

8. **Refresh.** Refresh your plan with something new. It could be a different tactic, setting, or career. Whatever it is, break out of the pattern you're in and try something new. Even if this new tactic doesn't yield positive results immediately, at the very least it will make you aware of the availability of your options.

9. **Networking.** Reach out to people in your social groups or those who share your life goal. You can do this a number of ways: check out local weight loss and fitness clubs, find a plethora people online, or talk to existing contacts that may have already succeeded in your goal.

   - *Having someone to voice your struggles, questions, and experience to will invigorate you to keep moving forward.*

10. **Action.** Taking action, despite doubts and setbacks, will further your progress. By moving on, despite any pessimistic thoughts, you will motivate yourself by the sheer momentum of doing *something* proactive to change your circumstances.

Whenever you feel like your progress has stalled, or you simply want some quick inspiration, look to these 10 powerful words and strategies to spur you on. You're sure to find something to get you back on track toward weight loss success!

Concluding Thoughts

Stop the excuses – get on with making change in your life:

You may already know that motivation is one of the keys that determine success or failure with weight loss or anything else. However, just knowing doesn't make it any easier to gain motivation.

If you feel that you're having trouble properly motivating yourself, it's time for you to act. Not tomorrow, but today.

Finding your motivation is something personal. The best way to find motivation is to explore your options and discover something that works for you.

101

Consider the following ways to motivate yourself today:

1. **Avoid just going through the motions.** One reason you may find it difficult to perform everyday tasks is that you get bored. Of course you're going to try to avoid something that you find tedious! You can combat this mentality by adding some depth to your thinking while you're engaging in tasks you dislike.

    - Brainstorm ways that you can complete the task in a more efficient manner. Then you can compete with yourself to see how quickly you can complete the task in the future. The quicker you get it done, the sooner you can move on to bigger and better things!

2. **Get spiritual.** Don't be afraid to get in touch with your spiritual side. Many people find it highly motivating! When you discover some answers to life's tough questions, it brings you clarity, and you may be more likely to work harder to achieve your desires.

3. **Set a goal.** You might lack motivation because you don't have a goal. If you aren't even sure what you're working towards, you'll have difficulty finding motivation.

    - If you have a large goal, *break up the goal into a series of small, achievable tasks* and set each task as a separate goal. This helps you maintain motivation because you're constantly achieving your goals. You can *see* the results of your hard work!

4. **Hold yourself accountable.** In order to ensure that you don't stray from your chosen path, evaluate your progress

every week or even every day. Determine how you can do better the next week.

- If you find that it's difficult to keep yourself accountable, **_don't be afraid to ask for help._** You may enjoy having others check up on you to make sure you stay on task.

5. **Think positive thoughts.** Negative thinking and lack of motivation go hand in hand. You can increase your motivation by concentrating on eliminating your negative thinking patterns. Replace negative feelings with optimism and positive thoughts and images.

- When you catch yourself feeling down, make an extra effort to seek the silver lining. It's always there. If you take the time to look hard enough, you'll find it.

6. **Make a change.** If you think you've tried everything and you still can't get motivated, perhaps you should consider a life change. Maybe there's a reason why you're feeling this way.

- If you don't feel motivated to work toward your major life goals, consider some alternatives that may be more in line with your true desires.

- If you're having trouble finding motivation for every-day chores, see if you can find a way to hire some help.

Always keep in mind that "the time is now." Put procrastination into your past and you'll feel happy and accomplished at the end of the day, instead of stressed out or regretful.

When you're motivated, life is more fulfilling.

Experts say that it takes 21 days to make a change in your habits. This book has 77 days of motivational quotes and images to get you going and keep you going. That means you have 3 sets of 21 days, plus another 2 weeks to get your act in gear. You can lose weight. You can achieve your goals. You can feel good about yourself.

Use these strategies to wake up your motivation and enjoy the difference!

Resources

Weight Control Information Network

http://win.niddk.nih.gov/publications/index.htm

Get practical tips and guidance on how to stick to a diet at

http://HowToStickToADiet.org

Discover how low carb diets can help you lose weight and improve your health at

http://EatLowCarbFoods.com

Made in the USA
Lexington, KY
19 September 2012